Can I Really Hear God?

Ron & Tonia Woolever

Shammah
Ministries

What People Have Said About

Can I Really Hear God?

Ron and Tonia Woolever's book *Can I Really Hear God?* is a well balanced, scriptural answer to this question. It is a book I can recommend without reservations.

> *Dr. B. J. Willhite*
> *President and Founder of National Call to Prayer*

The title of this book is one of the most pertinent questions confronting the Church in this hour. America is facing problems we have never faced before. As the authors so aptly point out in Chapter Two, God is a communicator. While this book deals primarily with the Christian's personal need to hear the Lord, it should also help us recognize the corporate need to hear Him. Every chapter in this book will touch your spirit and heart and help lead you into being a communicator with the heavenly Father. Your life will be immeasurably blessed as you learn more of Him in the sweet communion of His presence and learning to hear His precious voice. I highly recommend it.

> *John F. Moreland*
> *Euless, Texas*

Ron and Tonia have directed the focus of an intimate relationship with Father and Jesus to the essentials; talk with God and listen and obey God, tell God your needs and thank Him for His answers. Rich, rich, rich!

> *Rev. Hollis Kirkpatrick, Director*
> *Servants to the City*
> *Fort Worth, Texas*

In this valuable book, the Woolevers provide ample evidence that God still speaks. They offer clear practical counsel to anyone wanting to know how to hear God themselves. By applying the instruction offered here, anyone who follows Jesus will be able to begin living in the light of God's own illuminating voice.

> R. Leck Heflin, President
> PONTiS

Can I Really Hear God? is a priceless jewel. Ron and Tonia have a deep desire for the average Christian, in the average church, sitting on the average pew to be able to hear God's voice. This book is a well of refreshing news to the ones who want to hear God. I implore you to read this book as a devotional and as an excellent guide to hearing God.

> Rev. Paul E. Tsika, II, Pastor
> Plow On Ministries

The Woolevers have done such a great job in outlining a Biblical understanding of this important topic. In addition, they also give some practical instructions so we can apply this dynamic teaching into our daily lives. What a great resource!

> Dr. Dean Posey, Pastor
> First United Methodist Church
> Azle, Texas

This book is dedicated to Reverend
Lew Shaffer, a man who has
produced much fruit for the Lord
through his daily conversations
with Jesus, and who has taught so
many to hear the voice of God;

and

To our Lord Jesus Christ, who goes
to any extreme to talk with us.

Contents

Why Is It Hard to Pray?

If we are called by God, why is it so hard to pray?

This question has been asked by Christians for years and it grieves and troubles us deeply. So then, why is it so hard for Christians to pray?

Learning to pray is the first step in the process of talking with God. The Word makes it clear that the answer to everything in our lives is prayer mixed with faith. Paul wrote,

> Do not be anxious about anything, but in everything, by prayer and petition, with thanksgiving, present your requests to God. (Philippians 4:6).

Paul is telling us: seek the Lord about every area of your lives, things large and small, everything that concerns you. And thank Him ahead of time for hearing you and answering you. Note his emphasis: always pray first. We aren't to pray as a last resort after going to our friends, then the pastor or a spouse — finally ending up on our knees. NO, we are to seek the Lord first — before anyone.

It seems as if the Christian will turn to books, tapes, counselors, or logical reasoning to come up with life's answers; yet, rarely ever go to serious prayer, much less having serious interaction with God.

Standing against this fact in stark relief is the fact that the Bible stands as one long testimony that God hears the

cries of His children and answers them with unfailing love.
Consider just a few:

> The eyes of the Lord are on the righteous and his
> ears are attentive to their cry. (Psalm 34:15)

> The righteous cry out, and the Lord hears them;
> he delivers them from all their troubles. (Psalm
> 34:17)

> This is the confidence we have in approaching
> God: that if we ask anything according to his will, he
> hears us. And if we know that he hears us —
> whatever we ask — we know that we have what we
> asked of him. (1 John 5:14-15)

> If you believe, you will receive whatever you ask
> for in prayer. (Matthew 21:22)

> The prayer of a righteous man is powerful and
> effective. (James 5:16).

It is clear that the Father wants to have a two-way, conversational relationship with us:

> *God not only
> wants to hear us,
> He wants us to
> hear Him.*

> Call to me and I will
> answer you and tell you
> great and unsearchable
> things you do not know.
> (Jeremiah 33:3)

This should make it obvious that God not only wants to
hear us, He wants us to hear Him. It is also quite clear that

God is deeply troubled by the neglect of prayer among His people. Jeremiah wrote:

> *Does a maiden forget her jewelry, a bride her wedding ornaments? Yet my people have forgotten me, days without number.* (Jeremiah 2:32)

And he complains again in Jeremiah 16:12: *See how each of you is following the stubborness of his own evil heart instead of listening to me.*

Hebrews Chapter 10 has an incredible promise when it says that God's door is always open to us, giving us total access to the Father, an amazing grace given to all those who would enter into the new covenant of Jesus. In fact, we are commanded to draw near![1] The greatest promise of this new covenant is that we will all know God personally. This can only mean one thing: God is knowable. When we take lightly all that Jesus promised, we seem to be taking lightly the grace of God, and making it of no effect.

Recently, I heard a man of God give three reasons why most believers find it hard to pray, much less have a conversation with God. Let's discuss these reasons:

1. Some believers don't pray because they have a lukewarm love for the Lord!

Oh yes, they work hard for the church, hate sin, wouldn't accept false teaching, maybe are faithful in tithes (and even offerings), yet somehow in the midst of all their good works have forgotten their loving, disciplined walk with Jesus. They've gotten so busy doing "things" and "stuff"

---

[1] Hebrews 10:19-22

that the fiery, zealous enthusiasm which they originally had for Jesus has somewhere fallen by the wayside.

Just think about how this must hurt Jesus, who is to be our bridegroom. He wants moments with us all to himself. He wants to be intimate with us.

If your heart isn't continually being drawn to Jesus' presence, if you have no desire to know Him, the person who gave his life for you, then you simply don't love Him. Loving Jesus isn't just about doing "things." It is about pursuing, developing and maintaining a relationship, just as you would with any other person. Relationships only become strong and satisfying through intentional building, seeking, listening, sharing, exploring. Our relationship to God, a living Person, is no different.

Failure to pray, or even desire to pray, reveals a lack of interest or faith in pursuing this relationship. It is a sign that the heart believes there is not much worthwhile here to seek. It is a lack of faith in all the Bible has to say about the beauty of the Lord, the delights found in his presence, the sheer joy of walking with him and in his wise counsel. A true lover of God does not have to force himself to spend time with Him.

> *A true lover of God does not have to force himself to spend time with Him.*

2. Some don't pray because they have perverted their priorities!

A priority is the importance you place on something. For most, God remains at the bottom of the priority list.

Income, security, pleasure, corporate success, and family are at the top. The Lord doesn't want your leftovers — the little bits and pieces of time when you have only a moment to a toss up a quick prayer request. That isn't a sacrifice of prayer. It's a lame offering — I believe it pollutes His altar. Such prayers reduce God to something on your duty roster, like the relative you make yourself visit because it's the right thing to do or because you want to give the impression that you care.

Simple fact: no Christian will become faithful in prayer unless it becomes his or her first priority in life, above everything else — above family, career, leisure time, everything. Anything else is a perversion of the authentic relationship God desires to have with us.

3. Some don't pray because they've learned to live without prayer!

Many believers think all that's required of them is going to church, worship, paying their tithes, listening to the sermon, resisting sin, and doing their very best on a day-to-day level. Then, by doing this, God will be pleased with them.

This reasoning is part of the devil's greatest deception for the believer. He doesn't want you to know about intimacy; he doesn't want you to know that you can talk with and hear from the King of Kings and the Lord of Lords.

Satan has, for centuries, kept the believer from understanding their "covenant rights." The greatest gift of this thing called "salvation" is that you have been brought into a covenant relationship with your heavenly Father and He wants, more than anything else, to talk with and have fellowship with you, and help you become a genuine son or daughter whom He has raised and taught and loved and disciplined and comforted with His love.

Prayerless Christians are shallow in their faith, easy targets for false teachers, and quickly led astray from the true gospel. Prayerless Christians are always "learning" but never maturing!

Now we know why some won't pray, cannot pray, or simply refuse to pray. So then, let's look at some important reasons why prayer should be part of our day-to-day activities.

The great blessings of listening to God:

* God becomes very real; you sense His presence with you throughout the day.

* The Bible comes alive; its words leap off the pages to the heart.

* Faith becomes relevant in every moment, as you learn to live your life as a response to the Lord's presence.

* Prayer becomes a lively two-way conversation rather than a monologue or speech you make to God.

* You fall in love with the Lord the more you listen to Him and obey; this is "walking with God."

* Events less often catch you off guard or remain unexplained. Dangers and accidents are often averted. God often warns us beforehand, or explains and teaches after an event.

❋ You have more understanding of your life, which takes on purpose and direction because you understand and cooperate with what the Holy Spirit wants you to do.

❋ Corporate worship and private devotional times come alive. They become an exciting or deeply satisfying experience that the believer never dreads but always looks forward to because he has entered the real joy of knowing Jesus.

Can I Really Hear God?

The answer is YES if you are a born-again child of God who has entered into covenant with Him through the sacrificial death of Jesus Christ, and have invited His Holy Spirit to make His home in your heart. And in this chapter we hope to established firmly in your mind and heart that:

God is a person who communicates.

In the very beginning, the Lord spoke the creation into existence. After God created Adam, He visited him and conversed with him in the garden every day. More amazingly, even after Adam and Eve betrayed God's coveanant, died spiritually and were cast out of the Garden, God was still talking to them and to their children!

God told Noah to build an ark. A man would not spend 100 years building an ark to survive a flood on an earth where it has never rained before, unless he has heard from God. God communicated with Abraham when he was still a heathen in the land of Ur. Without a Bible, radio, CD's or Christian television, Abraham heard God's promise and entered into a covenant with him. He heard the voice of the invisible God and obeyed. Later, God made His voice known to each of Abraham's descendants.

David was a flesh and blood man like us, whose writings in the Psalms are laced with references to his experiences of

God's personal communication and intervention in his life. He learned about the love and character of God while out shepherding the sheep, without books, conferences or a Bible. All he had was the Holy Spirit, that same wonderful personal counselor and teacher Jesus promised would come live with every born-again believer. David's testimony was that it was hearing God's voice which kept him from acting like those around him, and thus helping him to display godly character:

> As for the deeds of men — by the word of your
> lips I have kept myself from the ways of the violent.
> (Psalms 17:4)

However you think these men heard God's voice, whether audibly, in mind or spirit, it is clear throughout scripture that God communicates to us. Throughout the Bible we find the phrase, *"the Lord said"* over 7,500 times in the Old Testament alone, translated from one of three Hebrew words which refer to something spoken, uttered, commanded, promised or discussed. Our God is a communicating God.

The Bible is consistent from Genesis to Revelation: in any age or dispensation, God's voice has been heard by (1) those He chose to hear it and (2) those who desired to hear it and were willing to respond to it! Isaiah said,

> The Sovereign Lord has given me an instructed
> tongue, to know the word that sustains the weary. He
> wakens me morning by morning, _wakens my ear to_
> _listen like one being taught._ (Isaiah 50:4)

Isaiah was a man like us, upon whom God put His Spirit. What Isaiah heard from God enabled him to reveal

God's broken heart to His rebellious people. God begged the people through Isaiah:

> Why spend money on what is not bread, and your labor on what does not satisfy? <u>Listen, listen to me</u>, and eat what is good, and your soul will delight in the richest of fare. (Isaiah 55:2)

> <u>Give ear and come to me; hear me,</u> that your soul may live. I will make an everlasting covenant with you, my faithful love promised to David. (Isaiah 55:3)

God spoke clearly only to those chosen few, and always he did so by means sending His own Spirit to be with them, to rest upon them, or live in them.

Most people have no trouble believing God spoke to Moses and the ancient prophets, but cannot believe that God would talk to "little old me." But the Bible makes it clear that God wants you to hear His voice even if you are the most insignificant Christian on earth. How do I know? The answer is found in the new covenant of Jesus and its provisions.

The Old Testament foretold, and the New Testament confirms, that through the death and resurrection of Jesus Christ, all are invited to unite with God in an everlasting covenant, in which God shares his life through the joining of His Spirit to the believer. The New Testament is filled with teaching on how this happens, what it will look like, and the kind of life it will result in.

The Covenant Jesus Died to Give Us

When Jesus was preparing to go to the cross, He lifted up the cup at the Passover service and said,

> *This cup is the new covenant in my blood, which is poured out for you. (Luke 22:20)*

Jesus didn't just die for our sins so we could go to heaven; His death made it possible for us to enter into a covenant relationship with God. The new covenant of Jesus specifically mentions the privilege of personally knowing and being taught by God:

> *This is the covenant I will make with the house of Israel after that time, declares the Lord. I will put my laws in their minds and write them on their hearts. I will be their God, and they will be my people. No longer will a man teach his neighbor, or a man his brother, saying, "Know the Lord," because they will all know me, from the least of them to the greatest. (Hebrews 8:10-11)*

Just before this, the author of Hebrews had written:

> *But the ministry Jesus has received is as superior... as the covenant of which he is mediator is superior to the old one, and it is founded on better promises. (Hebrews 8:6)*

There were several covenants before this one, and under each one God spoke to those He chose. Consider this: if God spoke to people personally under the old covenant, but now will not speak to us under the new one, we don't have a better covenant! The implication of these passages in

Hebrews could not be more clear: Jesus died to open up the way for us to know his Father as he knew the Father on earth: to be taught by him, loved by him, encouraged, mentored, fathered, disciplined — every benefit and facet of intimate relationship.

And consider this: Jesus said, *I only do what my Father tells me to do*, and *Greater works than I do, you will do*. Consequently, if Jesus did only what his father told him to do, and we're called to do even more, is it not logical that we too must be able to hear the voice of God as He did?

We each can personally hear the voice of the Lord as soon as we enter into the new covenant of Jesus by accepting his death in our place. Like an infant, we may have to grow up into understanding the words clearly, but from the time we are born again we can know the voice of the father because we are His children. If you are born again and have the Spirit of Jesus Christ in you, then you can hear His voice.

We aren't just invited to be saved, we are invited to share life with God.

We aren't just invited to be saved, we are invited to share life with God. Jesus, the "second Adam," came to restore the life that the first Adam lost for all mankind. This was God's plan and desire; why then, would he make it difficult for you to communicate with him? The problem is not one of unwillingness on his part; nor will you find any doctrine in the pages of the Bible that implies you must be perfect or mature to hear God's voice. On the contrary, Jesus said that unless we became more like little children —

trusting, simple, unconcerned about our performance — we would not be able to experience the Kingdom of heaven![1]

The Holy Spirit Reveals the Thoughts of God

In connection with hearing God's voice, the most enlightening instruction comes from Paul's first letter to the Corinthian church:

> However, as it is written: "No eye has seen, no ear has heard, no mind has conceived what God has prepared for those who love him"— but God has revealed it to us by his Spirit. The Spirit searches all things, even the deep things of God. For who among men knows the thoughts of a man except the man's spirit within him?

> In the same way no one knows the thoughts of God except the Spirit of God. We have not received the spirit of the world but the Spirit who is from God, that we may understand what God has freely given us. This is what we speak, not in words taught us by human wisdom but in words taught by the Spirit, expressing spiritual truths in spiritual words.

> The man without the Spirit does not accept the things that come from the Spirit of God, for they are foolishness to him, and he cannot understand them, because they are spiritually discerned....we have the mind of Christ. (1 Corinthians 2:9-16)

---

[1] Matthew 11:25-26.

Clearly, in this new covenant of Jesus, we have been given the privilege of knowing the thoughts of God. Yet even though God spoke to men and women in the times before Jesus up through the lives of those who wrote the Bible, many believe that after the apostles died off God just clammed up and said, "I am not talking to my children any more," as if he could be unfaithful in the matter of keeping his covenant promises!

How did Bible-believing Christians ever get to the place of doubting God's desire to interact with his people through living communication? A.W. Tozer remarked on this absurd concept in his excellent book, *The Pursuit of God:*

> *A silent God suddenly began to speak in a book and when the book was finished lapsed back into silence again forever. Now we read the book as the record of what God said when He was for a brief time in a speaking mood. With notions like that in our heads how can we believe? The facts are that God is not silent, has never been silent. It is the nature of God to speak.*[2]

What reason would God have for going silent on us? That we're not spiritual enough? We weren't spiritual enough for Jesus to die for us, but He did. Everything God gives us is a gift of His grace, based upon His desire to give it and His great love for us, not based upon our ability to earn or deserve it. It is by grace and faith we are saved. It is by grace and faith that we are filled with the Holy Spirit. It is also by grace and faith that we hear His voice.

The same God who made the universe by His word has given us ears to hear his voice — if we would only believe. Again, consider the wise words of A.W. Tozer, a man who heard God's voice:

---

[2] A.W. Tozer, <u>The Pursuit of God</u>, page 77. WingSpread Publishers, 2006

> ...God can be known in personal experience. A loving Personality dominates the Bible, walking among the trees of the garden and breathing fragrance over every scene. Always a living Person is present, speaking, pleading, loving, working and manifesting Himself whenever and wherever His people have the receptivity necessary to receive the manifestation. The Bible assumes as a self-evident fact that men can know God with at least the same degree of immediacy as they know any other person...we have in our hearts organs by means of which we can known God as certainly as we know material things through our familiar five senses...
>
> But why do the very ransomed children of God themselves know so little of that habitual, conscious communion with God which Scripture offers? The answer is because of our chronic unbelief. Faith enables our spiritual sense to function...[3]

The purpose of faith is not to just believe IN God, but to enable you to respond to the very real and present God you believe in!

God Communicates Any Way He Can

The purpose of this book is to reveal the overwhelming scriptural evidence that God wants to make His voice known to every believer. In doing so we must acknowledge the other ways God communicates. Moses wrote:

> If there is a prophet among you, I the Lord make myself known unto him in a vision; I speak to him in a dream. Not so with my servant Moses; he is faithful in all my house. I speak with him face to face, even

---

³ ibid, p. 48.

plainly, and not in dark sayings... (Numbers 12:6-8, NKJV)

Surely God's highest will is to speak to us "face-to-face," but when He cannot He will resort to dreams, visions, or "dark sayings." Dark sayings refers to any speech, parable, sign or coincidence which carries ulterior meanings. It can come through movies, books, teachings, authority figures, friends, or little children. It is something which grabs your heart and you know it is from the Lord. God speaks to us this way often. Jesus used dark speech when He said things like *I am the bread of life.*

God also speaks to us through circumstances, through the authorities placed over us, through friends and associates, through family members and, of course, through his written Word, the Bible. In fact, turning to God's written word is one of the best ways to open your spirit to hear Him, but He lives in His spoken words and is constantly speaking in those words. God will personally speak to you through them, as we will discuss further in a later chapter. Please read your whole Bible; there is no better way to acquire the vocabulary of the language God speaks and understanding His heart — a crucial matter in discerning the true hearing of His voice.

"Face-to-face" or "mouth-to-ear" communication requires the most risk on God's part, but it is still God's goal. He wants intimate fellowship with His children, the kind which can only come through sustained communication. God draws us to know Him through all the other means in order to get us to this place. Numbers 12:8 tells us that God spoke to Moses clearly; he obviously heard volumes of information in great detail from God, which we now have recorded in the first five books of the Bible!

How does God choose which way He will speak to us? By whatever way He knows our hearts are open to hear. But His highest will is to be able to communicate as a father does with his beloved child: clearly, with the sound of His personal voice instructing, comforting and guiding.

We Can and Must Know God Personally

You must hear His voice to enjoy all the benefits of this new covenant. Satan wants to keep this fact hidden so you won't fully enjoy the life God is giving you. He knows that hearing God's voice is the means by which you will destroy his evil works and release the will of God on earth as it is in heaven.

Jesus announced that this would be accomplished through the Holy Spirit coming to live in our hearts when He returned to the Father:

> But the Counselor, the Holy Spirit, whom the Father will send in my name, will teach you all things and will remind you of everything I have said to you. (John 14:26)

Now we have no excuses. We cannot point to another man or woman and blame them for how well we know our God. We cannot blame anyone else if we miss the life God is handing out to us, because no one can keep us from knowing God in this intimate way.

Remember what Hebrews 8:11 says? *"From the least to the greatest."* Everyone from the greatest — the most seasoned,

> He who belongs
> to God hears
> what God says.

spiritual person walking the face of the earth — to the least — the newest spiritual infant in the kingdom of God — can know God and be taught by Him. Jesus taught this to His disciples just before His crucifixion, explaining to them the importance of listening to the Holy Spirit, who would live right in them. Jesus said: *He who belongs to God hears what God says.*[4]

Why do so many not hear God's voice?

The main reason is they don't believe they can; it is a lack of faith. There is still widespread disbelief in this provision of the New Covenant. In our ministry work in the U.S. and overseas, we have found this to be one of the most critical and overlooked covenant blessings for the Christian. When we ask people for a show of hands in our meetings about whether they can hear God's voice in prayer, no matter which denominational (or non-denominational) persuasion, only about 10% will raise a hand of affirmation.

This is heartbreaking in light of what Jesus died to give us. We are not surprised that God doesn't seem very real to these people. Why is it that people can believe that God can be all-powerful, create the universe, save us from sin and change our character, but not make His voice known to us?

The problem is often that we do not doubt God's ability, but ours. We still think we have to achieve a certain level of spiritual maturity to hear His voice. We are so glad that Tonia was blissfully ignorant of that fact. She came to the

---

[4] John 8:47

Lord at the age of 29, had never read a page in the Bible or been exposed to the church or any doctrines. When she read, "My sheep know my voice" she didn't know better, so she did hear God's voice. And because she heard His voice, she heard His tender love words, was comforted in times of trouble, and was taught by Him. As a result, she grew very quickly in her knowledge of God. She has experienced times of not hearing God so well, but usually this happened because she moved away from the simple, childlike faith she had at the beginning.

You too, can hear His voice, if you only believe. We should beware of disbelieving God. In fact, not believing what God has said is the greatest sin we can commit against Him!

God uses consistent symbols throughout the Bible to give us simple but powerful teaching pictures. It is true that a picture is worth a thousand words. The symbol he has chosen for what comes from his mouth to us is water. Revelation 1:15 says of the Lord, "his voice was like the sound of rushing waters." Ephesians 5:26 claims that the Lord cleanses his church by washing her with the "water" of his words.

God could have chosen anything to represent His words. He could have chosen wind, or fire, or sunshine. Why did he choose water? We think it is for this reason: water flows, and in its flowing always finds its way into the lowest places, the humblest places, even into the sewers of life. When the snow on the mountaintop melts and becomes water, it never remains on the heights, it must flow down; and the lower it goes, the faster it flows.

Furthermore, science tells us that our very bodies are mostly water, and that we must have water to live. For this reason, thirst in our bodies is never satisfied for long. Jesus told the woman at the well, *"If you knew the gift of God…you would have asked him and he would have given you living water."*[5] God wants to water your soul, today and every day.

My Sheep Listen To My Voice

And when describing how the Lord would be as a shepherd to His people, Jesus said:

> The watchman opens the gate for him, and the sheep listen to his voice. He calls his own sheep by name and leads them out. When he has brought out all his own, he goes on ahead of them, and his sheep follow him because they know his voice. (John 10:3-4)

> I have other sheep that are not of this sheep pen. I must bring them also. They too will listen to my voice, and there shall be one flock and one shepherd. (John 10:16).

Finally, in John 10:27 Jesus said, My sheep listen to my voice; I know them, and they follow me.

Whenever a person in the Bible repeats something three times it is for the purpose of giving it the greatest possible emphasis. It means, you need to really pay attention to this, because this is an extremely important and unchangeable truth.

Notice that Jesus does not say, My sheep will know what to do because of the peace they feel. Or, My sheep will know how *to follow me by instinct.* If that is what Jesus meant, He would have said so. Jesus is never once reported to say, *I sense in my spirit that the Father wants me to....* No, he boldly declared he heard the Father's voice.

Most importantly Jesus teaches us that there is a clear and crucial connection between hearing God's voice and being able to follow Him. The goal of our life in Christ is not just to be a good person in this world hoping God will bless us, it is to walk with God and thereby naturally live in the blessings he has designed for us.

There is a big difference between puttering around this world as if God is sort of around and involved in some distant way, and engaging with him as a real teacher and counselor. In Psalm 32 David shares how he became physically ill and realized it was because he had sinned against God. After confessing his sin and asking God's forgiveness, the Lord said to him:

> *I will instruct you and teach you in the way you should go; I will counsel you and watch over you. Do not be like the horse or the mule, which have no understanding but must be controlled by bit and bridle or they will not come to you. Psalms 32:8-9)*

This verse also verifies that the Lord would much rather lead us by His voice than by unpleasant jerks — bad circumstances or people with a disciplinary or ungracious attitude towards us!

Communication is the strength of any relationship. Toni's beloved dog Lady went completely deaf when she was fourteen years old. She adored Toni and lived to be in her presence, but once Lady could no longer hear the sound of Toni's voice their relationship changed dramatically. Lady became much less responsive and obedient. In earlier times when Lady was stressed during a bath or a visit to the vet, Toni was able to sooth her with her voice; but when Lady lost her hearing Toni could no longer comfort her in this way. Lady became increasingly nervous, irritable and uncooperative.

Toni felt a deep sense of loss at the change in their relationship. Once Lady could no longer hear Toni's commands she did not obey her simply because she didn't know what Toni wanted her to do. Toni would have to get a leash and lead Lady on it to get her to do certain things. We realized how important the sound of Toni's voice had been in determining the quality of that relationship. It is no different with us and God, who asked David not to force Him to lead him in that way.

Jesus said, *Whoever has my commands and obeys them, he is the one who loves me.*[1] If we want to love God with all our heart, it is absolutely vital that we learn to know His voice. Clearly, the first step in being able to obey is revealed in Jesus' words, *whoever has my commands.* Once Lady lost her ability to hear, she no longer had Toni's commands. Though she loved Toni the same, her ability to show it was dramatically reduced when she could no longer obey.

Do you know what the Lord's will is for you?

Many have believed that everything they need to know about God's will for them is contained in the Bible. Consider this: we are commanded to pray about everything.[2]

[1] John 14:21
[2] Philippians 4:6

And to pray continually.[3]   We are told to find out what pleases the Lord[4]. Do you know what pleases the Lord? Do you know what the Lord's will is for you personally?

Each person's relationship with Jesus Christ is entirely unique. No one else can get together with the Lord to determine His personal will for you. In John 21:21-22 Peter asked Jesus what His intentions were for the Apostle John. Jesus essentially told him it was none of his business and said, *You follow me.* There are no two people on this earth who are called to walk with God exactly the same way. Each of us must know God's voice in order to personally follow Him.

Each of us must know God's voice in order to personally follow Him.

The Bible reveals His will for you regarding character, sin, and righteousness; but is His personal will exactly identical for every one of his millions of children? When your children were young, was your will for each of them identical every day? Was your will the same for your 17 year-old child as for your 4 year old? If so, you'd be a pretty ineffective parent!

To those of you who believe everything you need to know about God's will for you can be found in the Bible, we ask: does the Bible tell you who to marry? Does it tell you which job the Lord wants you to take or the perfect moment to ask for a raise? Does it tell you where your children should go to college?

---

[3] 1 Thessalonians 5:17
[4] Ephesians 5:10

If you think about it, you will realize that the will of God as revealed in Scripture is very general. It goes into great detail about how to conduct yourself in character and temperament, or how to know and respond to God, but does not answer the many major and minor questions which arise in your daily life. And if it contained all of God's will for you, why on earth would Paul have bothered to say, *Therefore do not be foolish, but understand what the Lord's will is!*[5] (Notice how Paul implies that those who do not understand God's will are foolish...)

In the next verse Paul says, *Be filled with the Spirit...* In building these two statements together Paul is encouraging us to develop a relationship with the Holy Spirit in which we can ask questions of the Father about His will and receive answers. This was clearly understood by Jesus' disciples. After personally teaching and discipling them He reassured them that the Holy Spirit would continue to teach them when He returned to heaven:

> *I have much more to say to you, more than you can now bear. But when he, the Spirit of truth, comes, he will guide you into all truth. He will not speak on his own; he will speak only what he hears, and he will tell you what is yet to come. He will bring glory to me by taking from what is mine and making it known to you. All that belongs to the Father is mine. That is why I said the Spirit will take from what is mine and make it known to you. (John 16:12-15).*

In addition, James says,

> *If any of you lacks wisdom, he should ask God, who gives generously to all without finding fault, and*

---

[5] Ephesians 5:17

it will be given to him. But when he asks, he must believe and not doubt, because he who doubts is like a wave of the sea, blown and tossed by the wind. That man should not think he will receive anything from the Lord... (James 1:5-7)

The New Living Translation renders this passage:

If you need wisdom — if you want to know what God wants you to do — ask him, and he will gladly tell you. He will not resent your asking. But when you ask him, be sure that you really expect him to answer, for a doubtful mind is as unsettled as a wave of the sea that is driven and tossed by the wind. People like that should not expect to receive anything from the Lord.

How can we be personally taught by God if we cannot hear His voice? Every born-again child of God receives the privilege of knowing the voice of the Father, the Shepherd, the Comforter, the Counselor, in this life. In fact, every promise of God, and all the power we need to be effective in our Christian lives, depends upon this communication where we come to know Him.

> *Every promise of God, and all the power we need to be effective in our Christian lives, depends upon this communication.*

Jesus didn't die just to save us from our sin, but to remove every barrier between us and God, so we can know him. In order to honor the great sacrifice of Jesus, we must fulfill our highest calling: is to know God intimately:

> This is what the Lord says: "Let not the wise man boast of his wisdom or the strong man boast of his strength or the rich man boast of his riches, but let him who boasts boast about this: that he understands and knows me..." (Jeremiah 9:23-24)

Would you be willing to boast that you know and understand the heart of God? Few would, yet obviously God wants to be known by His creation, and has done everything to make it possible for us. It is impossible to know God through the experiences of others. And there is absolutely nothing which can hinder our growing knowledge of God, save for our own laziness or lack of faith.

There are two main ways we get to know God: the first is by reading and becoming familiar with the whole Bible, not just a few favorite verses. The Bible reveals the character, purposes and ways of God. It is a detailed revelation of who God is and helps us learn to distinguish His language or voice from our own thoughts or those of the devil.

Please find a translation of the Bible you can understand and read it every day. If you read just a half hour each day, you could read the whole Bible in less than a year. We are continually amazed at how few Christians actually study their Bibles.

The second way we get to know God is through developing an interactive relationship in which He not only hears our voice in prayer, but we hear His.

The Difference Between God's Word and God's Word

Some people believe that "God's Word" always refers to the written scriptures. The New Testament writers used two words to refer to the words that come to us from God. One word is *logos*, and refers to teaching. It comes from the primary root *lego* (yes, as in the building blocks for kids) which means to lay forth in words by a systematic discourse, to build line upon line. *Logos* describes teaching, whether written, as in the Bible, or spoken. It is education.

God gave *logos* teaching (about Himself and His laws) by speaking it first to Moses and the prophets, who later recorded it in written form. Jesus gave the crowds of listeners *logos* teaching.

The second word used in the New Testament is *rhema*, which means an utterance, something spoken. It comes from a root word which means to flow or pour forth like water. Strong's Dictionary defines *rhema* as "that which is or has been uttered by the living voice."

Rhema refers to the personal words spoken in the ears of our spirit as it flows from the heart of God. This word is used in Matthew 4:4 when Jesus says *Man does not live on bread alone but by every word (rhema) that comes from the mouth of*

God. It is used in Luke 1:38 when Mary says, *Be it unto me according to your word (rhema), Lord,* referring to that thing the angel just told her from God.

In Ephesians 5:26 when it says that Jesus cleanses the church by the "washing with water through the word," *rhema* is the Greek word employed, which verifies the concept of the personal words of God flowing to us, and how different this can be than just receiving his general teaching (*logos*).

Remember the sword of the Spirit we are to use against our spiritual enemies in Ephesians 6:18? *Rhema.* So our offensive weapon to use against the devil's schemes is the personal instruction given us by the Holy Spirit. How many Christians have suffered because they pulled some verse out of the Bible to use against their spiritual enemy that may have been good and true, but totally inappropriate for the spiritual battle at hand?

The Bible is both *logos* and *rhema.* As it sits on your desk, it is *logos,* God's teaching revelation to us all. But when you pick it up and read it under the guidance of the Holy Spirit and He quickens a certain verse to you, applying something personally to your life, it becomes *rhema,* a living utterance from God.

One morning many years ago as Tonia was reading the following verses, the Lord spoke to her and said, *I personally promise this to you:*

> *The righteous will flourish like a palm tree, they will grow like a cedar of Lebanon; planted in the house of the Lord, they will flourish in the courts of our God. They will still bear fruit in old age, they will stay fresh and green.* (Psalm 92:12-14).

Needless to say, she liked that promise very much, and in her journal entry that day she recorded that the Lord added that she would have to do her share by taking care of her body. This is an example of the Lord taking the written words in the Bible and making it a *rhema* word to her. However, many years later the Lord said to Tonia, *Remember that promise I made you about staying "fresh and green" as you age? Well, I can't keep it if you keep drinking coffee and caffeine!*

If Tonia had heard only the promise and not the later warning (and quit drinking caffeine) she likely would have suffered health problems and wondered why God did not keep his Word. All relationships are living things; they depend upon continuing communication to avoid misunderstanding and keep it right.

Logos is a word that might be true any time, like teaching about obedience to God. You could say it to a crowd and it would be appropriate for them all. But *rhema* is when God says, *You need to do this thing today.* It is personal and relevant for this specific moment and circumstances in your life. It might not be relevant any other day or time. *Rhema* is what flows from one person to another as a personal communication.

Logos is what God wants; *rhema* is what God wants <u>of me</u>. *Logos* is the right way to act; *rhema* is <u>the right thing for me to do</u> in this specific situation. *Logos* is education; *rhema* is revelation. We can explain the difference like this: a student may can go to school and be taught that it is right to serve in his community. That is education. But when his father says, *This weekend you need to do volunteer work at the public library*, then he has received revelation from "on high" (the authority over him) showing him when to specifically apply what he has been taught. And, as is the nature with all *rhema* (that which is uttered by a living voice), it comes with the expectation of a personal response.

Without revelation (wisdom and strategic information) we can misapply our education. In fact, education without revelation can get us in a lot of trouble, especially in our life with God, who is the invisible but supreme authority over our lives. This is clearly pictured in the sad but profound difference between a Pharisee and Jesus — both determined to uphold the Word of God.

Reading the Bible from cover to cover, you find things that seem to conflict. On one hand, you are told to love an enemy; on the other, to shun those who do not live according to God's righteous laws. How do you know when to do what? That is what *rhema* is for. It is the personal instruction that flows from God's Spirit to my spirit in the moment I need it.

The fact that Jesus is our righteousness means more than just receiving the benefit of his righteousness by association; it also means that he is the ever-available guide to righteousness for every situation in our daily lives. As we hear and obey the Lord, we naturally walk in righteousness. How many people have misapplied God's *logos* Word over the centuries, going so far astray from the heart of God because they did not listen to His own counsel!

> *How much more should we seek the Father's wisdom – if the very Son of God did so?*

Jesus once said His ministry was effective because, *I only do what the Father says.* Jesus judged or responded to everything by listening to the *rhema* words of his Father. Isaiah 11:2-4 promised, and Jesus verified,[1] that he would judge nothing by what he

---

[1] See John 8:15-16.

saw or heard with his physical eyes and ears. How much more should we seek the Father's wisdom – if the very Son of God did so?

People marveled at Jesus. He had the same scriptures the Pharisees did, but when he applied them, it was obvious he did so with stunning wisdom and true authority. He obviously sought the counsel — the *rhema* — of the Holy Spirit at every turn.

For instance, when the woman caught in the act of adultery was brought before Jesus, if he had only gone by the *logos* word of his father He would have stoned her with the rest of the crowd. Certainly he was the only one without sin in the crowd who had a right to do so, yet he did not. In this case the Holy Spirit counseled him to say something that effectively judged the sin of the whole crowd, not just the woman, which was the most righteous thing to do in that moment.

God knows how to balance perfect love and justice; we do not. He alone knows the truth and motivation of every heart present, knows the end from the beginning of a situation. It is only through hearing His voice that we will be truly like Him and understand how to walk wisely by His Word in this world.

To summarize, *logos* is teaching; *rhema* is personal counseling. *Logos* is right for everyone; it is a truth like two plus two equals four. *Rhema* is right for me, and takes into account all the factors in my life and other lives touching mine right now. When Jesus stood on the hillside and taught, He gave forth the *logos* of God. When He personally

> *Logos is teaching; rhema is personal counseling.*

took Peter aside and counseled him, it was His personal *rhema*.

The Bible tells us everything we need to know about God, about how to be saved, what the kingdom of God is like. The Bible is God's *logos* truth to all of us. It does not tell a person who to marry, what job to take, where to go to school, how to care for their body or how to pray for a specific person or situation. For all these things…for understanding the personal path God wants to lead you on in finding your life with Him, you need God's personal *rhema*, the revelation of His will for you. When you are at a crossroads in your life, you have His promise that:

> *Whether you turn to the right or to the left, your ears will hear a voice behind you, saying, "This is the way; walk in it." (Isaiah 30:21)*

We all need to know this voice to walk the personal path of abundant life Jesus promised us.

Abundant Life Comes From Personally Hearing God

Christians easily become disillusioned about God when their life in Christ does not turn out to be what they expected. In counseling we often hear complaints that people don't know God's will, don't feel His love, don't understand Him at all. They are battered by the enemy and overcome by their own weakness. It seems their lives bear small resembled to all the promises the Bible makes about abundant life in Christ.

In our quest for abundant life, we often look in the wrong place. We look for the material blessings God has promised and expect a certain success to frame our lives. Jesus' promise of abundant life does not mean you will never have problems; He assures Christians that trouble will come at times to every life. But without doubt, we are promised an abundant life and many wonderful and amazing blessings to attend our knowledge of God, both material and spiritual. God wants to give many good gifts to his children; that's just the way he is.

Without negating these promises from God in any way, it is good to understand above all, the abundant life Jesus promised offers to satisfy man's deep and perpetual hunger for righteousness, peace and joy.

> *The abundant life Jesus promised offers to satisfy man's deep and perpetual hunger for righteousness, peace and joy.*

This abundant life is offered to us at all times, regardless of what we are going through. Jesus said that abundant life consisted in knowing God personally, through experiencing his presence, his voice, his company, his fellowship:

Now this is eternal life: that they may know you, the only true God, and Jesus Christ, whom you have sent. (John 17:2)

In fact, Jesus warned us:

The thief comes only to steal and kill and destroy; I have come that they may have life, and have it to the full. (John 10:10)

As we shall show in this chapter, there is a vital connection between the promise of life to the full and hearing God's voice personally.

Every person who is born again is promised a new life, but few realize that this new life is actually hidden from you like a great treasure waiting to be discovered. Scripture says it can be found in only one place, but tells us where to look: *For you died,* says Colossians 3:3, *and your life is now hidden with Christ in God.* In other words, this life is hidden in the living person of Jesus Christ, and you will only experience it as you relate to Him.

Actually, this is true of any relationship. Only as you develop greater and greater intimacy with a person will they begin to open up and give to you the best that is within them. As a people with free will, we all choose when we will personally share the treasures in our souls with another person, that which is "abundant life" in us. It is one of the divine privileges of relationship, whether the person in question is your spouse or Jesus.

Jesus acknowledged these truths when He said, *I am the bread of life*, and *The one who "feeds" on me will live*. He was referring to the transference which occurs between people in intimate relationship. In a close relationship you partake of their personality and character. Our bread is Jesus; we are nourished to life as we come to know Him, and that knowing only comes through communication, particularly hearing the voice of His Spirit speak to the ears of our spirits.

Abundant Life Is Entering God's Rest

There is a thread of exquisite promise running throughout the Bible: that of entering God's rest. The concept of rest is multi-faceted in the Bible, which variously portrays it as (1) freedom from disease, (2) contentment of heart, (3) safety from one's enemies. Our favorite is the way in which rest often used in Scripture to refer to a home for one's heart, such as one finds in the intimacy and security of a permanent relationship like marriage.[1]

In many Old Testament places God invites us to enter His rest, and it is this last concept to which He refers: the rest that comes from a secure relationship where you are loved in an unfailing, deeply satisfying way. It is to this life that the Lord calls us, a fact most clearly described in the third and fourth chapters of Hebrews

---

[1] Ruth 1:9

The author of Hebrews describes how God tried to lead the Hebrew children in the wilderness into His rest, which for them was the Promised Land God had prepared for them, filled with houses they hadn't built and vineyards they had not planted and countless other blessings. Yet entering this land depended upon their developing a closeness to God in true covenant relationship, wherein they knew and relied upon the faithful heart of God. This would require them to live by their commitment to listen to and respond to God, but when He tried to speak to them, they were afraid to hear His voice for themselves. Instead, they begged God to just tell Moses what He wanted them to know. [2] So Moses would go into his tent and meet with God, who spoke with him *face-to-face, as a man speaks to his friend.* [3]

Because of this Moses came to know and understand the heart of God, but the people did not. When it was time to go into the Promised Land, and the people discovered there were powerful men they would have to fight, they refused, and shrunk back in fear. When Moses wrote of this episode, he reported that the people actually accused God of trying to lead them to their harm! [4] This broke God's heart and angered Him deeply. Since the people did not know God intimately nor trust in His love, they rebelled and did not enter God's rest.

The author of Hebrews warns us to consider what happened to them and learn from it:

> *So, as the Holy Spirit says: "Today, if you hear his voice, do not harden your hearts as you did in the rebellion, during the time of testing in the desert,*

---

[2] Exodus 20:19
[3] Exodus 33:11
[4] Deuteronomy 1:26-28.

*where your fathers tested and tried me and for forty
years saw what I did. That is why I was angry with
that generation, and I said, 'Their hearts are always
going astray, and they have not known my ways.' So
I declared on oath in my anger, 'They shall never
enter my rest.'"* (Hebrews 3:7-11)

The writer continues by saying to today's Christian:

*Therefore, since the promise of entering his rest
still stands, let us be careful that none of you be
found to have fallen short of it. (Hebrews 4:1).*

The promised land of the ancient Hebrews symbolizes
two things for us: our abundant life on this earth, and the
promise of living eternally with God in heaven when the
physical body dies. To fall short of entering God's rest is to
fail to enter God's promised abundant life here or in heaven.
That abundant life may mean many things, and different
things to different people as they interact with God;   Jesus
summed it up for all when he described it as *personally
knowing God.*

In Hebrews three and four the writer emphasizes the
thought of hearing God's voice "today" by repeating it a
total of five times! Today, today, today, if you hear God's
voice, don't harden your heart in unbelief! He finishes by
saying,

*It still remains that some will enter that rest, and
those who formerly had the gospel preached to them
did not go in, because of their disobedience. Therefore
God again set a certain day, calling it Today, when a
long time later he spoke through David, as was said
before: "Today, if you hear his voice, do not harden
your hearts." (Hebrews 4:6-7).*

The hard heart: deaf, unresponsive, indifferent.

These verses show that failure to listen to and respond to the Lord leads to the hardening of our hearts. Most people do not think of themselves as having a hard heart, usually viewing it as a state of being against God in some determined manner. But the Bible characterizes a hard heart most commonly as a desensitized heart, one that is deaf, unresponsive, or indifferent.

If we don't hear God, we can't obey Him. As long as we are not obeying, we experience neither God's rest nor His unfailing love. If you are unable to rest in the unfailing love of God, it is probably because you have not entered the intimacy with Him that comes from hearing His voice. While our introduction to God's unfailing love begins with faith, it was never his intention that we have to keep convincing ourselves that he loves us. No, he invites us to enter into the same knowing of the Father's love that Jesus experienced — he, the firstborn of many brothers[5] — through the sound of the Father's voice, made possible by the Holy Spirit indwelling.

How often we have been comforted by the voice of the Lord in a moment of discouragement by hearing Him say, "*I am with you!*" How often stress possesses us until we ask the counsel of God and He tells us something that changes everything about how we look at the problem. Tonia remembers stressing over missing writing deadlines, feeling like a failure and assuming God was upset with her. When she asked God to forgive her, He gently said, *I didn't put those deadlines on you, you did. You are right on time as far as I'm concerned!*

---

[5] Romans 8:29

Why would someone harden their heart against hearing God? The answer is that we don't want to be responsible for hearing (and therefore obeying) God. What He asks of us might not be what we want. Instinctively, we realize we are better off not to know God's will than to know what it is and ignore Him.

God complained to Jeremiah: *Who will listen to me? Their ears are closed so that they cannot hear. The word of the Lord is offensive to them; they find no pleasure in it.*[6]

Why is the word of the Lord offensive to us? We are afraid that the will of God will be unpleasant for us.

> *Instinctively, we realize we are better off not to know God's will than to know what it is and ignore Him.*

We find no pleasure in it because we're afraid that if we listen to God, we won't get what we want. We're afraid God will send us to Africa. We fear He will tell us to give up chocolate. We're afraid he will ask us to pray for an hour a day. We dread hearing Him tell us to be kind to the person who hurt us. We are afraid God will tell us that we have messed up.

We are afraid to hear what God wants to say because we love our freedom and independence. Hearing God forces us to face our real surrender or lack of it as we relate to Him.

Underlying every possibility is our failure to trust in God and His unfailing love. We fear that somehow He won't love us as well as we can ourselves. God is still on trial with us and we're not quite sure He's motivated to lead us to life.

---

6 Jeremiah 6:10

Think about this: the Bible says that God is love. It says from beginning to end that He loves us so much He has pursued us and gave everything to make a way to live with us forever, and He didn't want to wait until we got to heaven, He lives within us now, by His own choice. He passionately loves us. In fact, God's commands are His love coming to you! His word is His will, and His will is to love you.

> His word is His will, and His will is to love you!

Hearing clearly comes more easily to the one who trusts God completely. There is no fear, because love throws fear out the window. We don't have to be afraid to hear anything God has to say to us. God is good. His command is good. It is perfect for you. It is the expression not only of His righteousness, but His unfailing love for you.

Knowing this, when we hear God's commands we have no dread of obedience. There is no need to ask, *Is this right? Will it hurt me?* These thoughts no longer trouble us, because it is settled in the heart: *God loves me. His commands are His love coming to me.* We can obey without question, not because we are spiritual giants, but because we are trusting children. And in this we find the secret to causing God to delight in us:

> *...the Lord delights in those who fear him, who put their hope in his unfailing love. (Psalms 147:11).*

Put your hope in God's unfailing love. Then when you pray and hear God's will, you don't have to stop and wrestle with dread. If you trust God, you will be at peace and will not stumble over doubt, fear, or selfishness on your path.

God will no longer be on trial with you once you cease doubting His motives or intentions.

Once you have no fear of anything this perfect parent would ask of you, you will find it possible to let go of your own desires. They are easily dropped to the side because you know they are shabby next to the plans God has for you: *No eye has seen, no ear has heard, no mind has conceived what God has prepared for those who love him...*[7] You will realize God can love you better than you can love yourself.

David had an awesome revelation of the love and goodness of God. He wrote Psalm 119 to lavish upon the Lord his delight in His commands:

> *I run in the path of your commands, for you have set my heart free... Direct me in the path of your commands, for there I find delight... I delight in your commands because I love them... All your commands are trustworthy... How sweet are your words to my taste, sweeter than honey to my mouth!*[8]

We must hear God in order to experience His love to the fullest.

Before going to the cross Jesus said to His disciples:

> *As the father has loved me, so have I loved you. Now remain in my love. If you obey my commands, you will remain in my love, just as I have obeyed my Father's commands and remain in his love. I have told you this so that my joy may be in you and that your joy may be complete. (John 15:9-11)*

---

[7] 1 Corinthians 2:9
[8] Verses 32, 35, 47, 86, 103

This is one of the most crucial verses in the Bible, for it gives us the key to experiencing the fullness of God's immeasurable love. To live in His love, we must walk in His will. To walk in His will, we must understand what that will is; and to know His will, we must hear His voice!

Is your joy complete? Jesus experienced great joy in His knowledge of the Father and said in essence, *I want the same joy I have to be in you. And it is for this reason that I say, you should have and obey the commands of God!*

Furthermore, Jesus also revealed that having and responding to the *rhema* counsel of God is the key to achieving fruitfulness:

> *I am the vine; you are the branches. If a man remains in me and I in him, he will bear much fruit; apart from me you can do nothing. If anyone does not remain in me, he is like a branch that is thrown away and withers; such branches are picked up, thrown into the fire and burned.*
>
> *If you remain in me and my words (rhema) remain in you, ask whatever you wish, and it will be given you. This is to my Father's glory, that you bear much fruit, showing yourselves to be my disciples.* (John 15:5-8)

The fruit of the Spirit is not like a magic cloak that is dropped on you when you ask Jesus into your life, instantly changing your character. The fruit of the Spirit is produced only as you respond to the Holy Spirit's leading in your life. The Spirit himself has a voice, and is trying to communicate with you all the time.

We cannot get life from the world. We must reach out to heaven for it. Moses said we need God's words for life far more than we do the physical food we eat:

> He humbled you, causing you to hunger and then feeding you with manna, which neither you nor your fathers had known, to teach you that man does not live on bread alone but on every word that comes from the mouth of the Lord. (Deuteronomy 8:3).

In the original Hebrew of this verse, there is actually no word for "word;" the translators added it for clarification. A literal translation would simply say that man lives on that which goes forth from the mouth of the Lord.

We have a plaque hanging in our home that says, *God gives His best to those who give the choice to Him.* We don't know who wrote it, but we know it is God's plan, as verified in Scripture:

> If my people would but listen to me, if Israel would follow my ways, how quickly would I subdue their enemies and turn my hand against their foes! Those who hate the Lord would cringe before him, and their punishment would last for ever. But you would be fed with the finest of wheat; with honey from the rock I would satisfy you. (Psalms 81:13-16).

The Wonderful Counselor

Christians who don't believe God communicates with them struggle through life without the benefit of His personal guidance. James 1:8 says of such people, *They can't make up their minds. They waver back and forth in everything they do.* (New Living Testament)

Instead of being filled continually with the Spirit and the knowledge of God's love, joy and peace, too many believers struggle continually with worry, stress, anxiety or depression. The voice of Wisdom in Proverbs Chapter Eight says to us:

To you, O men, I call out; I raise my voice to all mankind. You who are simple, gain prudence; you who are foolish, gain understanding. Listen, for I have worthy things to say; I open my lips to speak what is right. (verses 4-6)

Choose my instruction instead of silver, knowledge rather than choice gold, for wisdom is more precious than rubies, and nothing you desire can compare with her. (verses 10-11)

Now then, my sons, listen to me; blessed are those who keep my ways. Listen to my instruction and be wise; do not ignore it. Blessed is the man who listens to me, watching daily at my doors, waiting at my doorway. For whoever finds me finds life and receives favor from the Lord. But whoever fails to find me harms himself; all who hate me love death. (verses 8:32-36).

Who is this voice of wisdom, and how do we listen to it? According to Colossians 2:3 this voice has its source in Jesus Christ, ...in whom are hidden all the treasures of wisdom and knowledge. This is the spirit of Jesus Christ, the one whom Isaiah said would be called the "Wonderful Counselor." [1]

God knows that living out a relationship here on earth with an invisible God is a daunting task, so He sent us a helper. When Jesus was preparing to return to the Father's side in heaven, He promised to send the Holy Spirit, a counselor who would be with us forever and would keep us advised us as to His will. Jesus reassured His followers that it was good that He was going away, because He could only be in one place at a time, but the Holy Spirit would be with all believers all the time:

> And I will ask the Father, and he will give you another Counselor to be with you for ever — the Spirit of truth. The world cannot accept him, because it neither sees him nor knows him. But you know him, for he lives with you and will be in you. (John 14:16-17)

> When the Counselor comes, whom I will send to you from the Father, the Spirit of truth who goes out from the Father, he will testify about me. (John 15:26).

---

[1] Isaiah 6:9

When we think of going to a counselor, we picture sitting down and talking out our problems, asking questions, getting advice. We think of interaction and dialogue about the issues that concern us. We would never go to someone who only listens and never offered to help us with our problems.

This is exactly what the Holy Spirit's role is in our lives. A counselor counsels. Webster's Dictionary defines counsel as "advice given

> *When we think of going to a counselor, we picture sitting down and talking out our problems, asking questions, getting advice.*

especially as a result of consultation; a policy, or plan of action, or behavior." It defines advice as "an opinion or instruction given for directing the judgment or conduct of another."

Years ago our marriage failed, and we were headed for divorce, in spite of being Bible-believing people in ministry who love Jesus! We had been fighting for months, and at the end of a horrible argument in which we both vowed to get a divorce, Tonia drove off with Ron shouting after her, *Don't ever come back!* She didn't make it very far, however, because she was crying so hard. In the parking lot of a nearby store Tonia poured her heart out to God until she could quiet herself. Then she asked the Lord what to do. The answer that came back was, *If you love me, go home to Ron.*

That was a tough thing for Tonia to hear, because at that moment the thought of going back into what had become a miserable marriage was more than she could bear. But she reasoned that she could trust God to give her life in what He commanded, and she wanted to prove she loved God by obeying Him, so she returned home, on the basis of these two factors alone.

It turned out that Ron also had the same experience with the Holy Spirit, who had told him, *If you love me, let Tonia come back.* Ron had no more hope in the marriage to succeed, but he also trusted God's voice and wanted to prove his love.

To two people who felt as if their marriage had become hopelessly painful, hearing God say to go back into it was not what we wanted to hear. However, we obeyed God because we had come to believe in the fact that He is always motivated by His unfailing love for us, by his desire to give us abundant life.

It was not easy to start over, but we did something we had never done before: we turned to the Lord — individually and together — for His counsel on how to love and live with one another. He personally counseled each of us right into a great marriage. And His counsel was different to each of us, for Tonia needed to learn different things in order to be the wife God was calling her to be, than Ron needed to be as the husband.

Though we both had been filled with the Spirit and prayed regularly, we had never put God right in the middle of our relationship as a counselor. (At the direction of the Lord we also went to a counselor "with skin on," who did help; but the most profound counsel we received was from God himself.) We love our Wonderful Counselor, who caused us to laugh, cry, and marvel at his personal wisdom for us.

We have experienced the blessing of God's personal counsel again and again. While admitting that hearing God's voice presents a frequent challenge to our trust, we cannot imagine what our lives would be like without it; only that they would be very different, in a negative way. When we listen and obey, we live truly abundant lives. We could write another book of testimonies about how our relationships and work have been changed by hearing God.

When we first met the woman our son married, Tonia was a bit put off by her, juding her to be somewhat arrogant and unteachable. But when Tonia asked the Lord to show her the truth about Sharon, He said: *Her heart is like the softest piece of clay in my hands, and she is hungry to learn.* This was the opposite of Tonia's impression, and it changed her attitude completely. Responding to what the Lord told her about Sharon rather than trust her own impression, Tonia formed a wonderful relationship with her right from the start and found that all God told her was true. How different their relationship might have been if Tonia had acted upon her own impressions. Tonia had totally misjudged a desire on Sharon's part to make a good impression on her new in-laws.

In another instance, our son Shawn ran away from home when he was a teenager, moving in with another family in our small town. Ron's reaction was to insist that until Shawn repented of his rebellion, no communication would happen between us. Tonia, with her soft mother's heart, felt this was too harsh and grew increasingly angry and resentful towards Ron over this decision. This caused a heartbreaking division between them on top of the anguish they were already experiencing. But when Tonia finally asked the counsel of the Lord, He told her, *Ron is doing exactly what I want done. This is the right thing and I want you to stand by him and trust us both in this.* Hearing this, Tonia could not continue to feel as she did because the Holy Spirit had changed her mind.

Though it hurt Tonia not to have any contact with Shawn, she committed to respond to what God said with all her heart. in doing this, God set her free of all resentment and she asked Ron to forgive her. This restored the closeness they needed so much at this time, and because they now had each other's comfort they were able to endure the nine-month separation with grace and peace.

Tonia was amazed that even in the presence of heartache over her son, her life-joy and abundance of heart returned. What God told her had set her free of resentment and restored the unity of her marriage. How different this season would have been without the Holy Spirit's counsel!

Jesus said in John 8:32, *You shall know the truth, and the truth shall set you free.* Our experience has been that just knowing the truth in the Bible has not set us free, but being able to apply the truth (given from the mouth of God) has set us free again and again from the trap of the devil. With his word comes power, and nothing is impossible when one embraces and applies the words God has spoken.[2]

Psalm 119:130-131 says,

> *The unfolding of your words gives light; it gives understanding to the simple. I open my mouth and pant, longing for your commands.*

When God speaks, His words give light; we can see the real truth about a situation. We know the right(eous) thing to do in this moment, in this circumstance, regarding this person.

---

[2] Luke 1:37 (*Nothing is impossible with God*) reveals this in the original Greek as it contains the word "*rhema*" and is more literally translated "It is impossible for any word of God to be without power."

The one who makes this incredible treasure available to us from God is the Holy Spirit. We are so grateful for the Holy Spirit, of whom Jesus said,

> *When God speaks, His words give light; we can see the real truth about a situation.*

> *But when he, the Spirit of truth, comes, he will guide you into all truth. He will not speak on his own; he will speak only what he hears, and he will tell you what is yet to come. (John 16:13)*

This is exactly what happened to the believers in the book of Acts. Throughout this exciting book we see the Holy Spirit speaking, guiding, warning, encouraging, teaching. Receiving communication from God was so vitally important for those first Christians who had to learn how to live without Jesus in the flesh.

It is foolish to think that the Spirit guides us any differently than He did the believers in the book of Acts, who were the first people to be saved and filled with the Spirit. But this is exactly what the devil has convinced believers of in the centuries since then. His greatest victory is that we have believed him! It is primarily through convincing people they cannot hear God that Satan has accomplished his goal: to steal the fulfillment of God's promises from us, to destroy God's life in us and resist the advancing kingdom of God.

The devil loves this because he knows that to hear God personally is to be able to walk in step with God and to know His thoughts. When we know God's will, we can pray in agreement with it, and thereby release His will on earth as it is in heaven.

Hearing and obeying God is the source of our strength against the devil.

Jesus once said that even though Satan was coming at Him with all the force of hell to defeat Him, he would not be able to touch Him. However, it is important to note that in this He did not claim to be invincible because He was the Son of God, or by possessing a spiritual super strength. Instead, He attributed His immunity from the devil's power to one thing only: He listened to and obeyed His Father:

> ... *the prince of this world is coming. He has no hold on me, but the world must learn that I love the Father and that I do exactly what my Father has commanded me. (John 14:30-31)*

As we hope the above examples show, we have the same potential for immunity from the devil's schemes, through the same means. Paul verified this when he wrote:

> *For though we live in the world, we do not wage war as the world does. The weapons we fight with are not the weapons of the world. On the contrary, they have divine power to demolish strongholds. We demolish arguments and every pretension that sets itself up against the knowledge of God, and we take captive every thought to make it obedient to Christ. (2 Corinthians 10:3-5).*

When we obeyed God's thoughts, we defeated the enemy's plan to destroy our marriage. When Tonia traded her thoughts for God's about Sharon, it destroyed the devil's plans to thwart Sharon's discipleship in the things of Christ. Today Sharon is a powerful woman of God. When Tonia took her thoughts of resentment over Shawn and made them obedient to Christ, the devil's plans to tear the whole family apart were defeated. Shawn later returned to both the Lord and us in repentance and our relationship became better than ever.

It is less accurate to say that God gives us life than to say that He, with His thoughts and power, IS our life. God said to His people:

> This day...I have set before you life and death, blessings and curses. Now choose life, so that you and your children may live and that you may <u>love the Lord your God, listen to his voice</u>, <u>and hold fast to him. For the Lord is your life</u>... (Deuteronomy 30:19-20)

The devil's greatest tool in his scheme to kill, steal from and destroy the believer is to keep him or her from knowing God personally. He lies constantly to us, telling us we cannot hear God's voice, or filling us with fear that we'll hear the devil or mess it all up somehow. Unfortunately, many Christians have more faith in their ability to hear from the devil than to hear from God. As someone wisely said once, "Fear is actually faith in the devil!"

God is bigger than any mistakes we might make, and is quite clearly far more willing to take a chance on our human frailty than we are.

Hearing God's Voice is the Key to Authoritative, Effective Intercession

Anyone who aspires to intercession should consider this: when we pray, do we pray as we wish, out of our own understanding, or do we ask God how to pray for others? A very important part of what it means to "pray in the Spirit" is to pray as the Spirit directs. Praying that comes out of our own "wisdom" may completely miss the mark.

Jesus taught this principle in John 14:14-15:

> *You may ask me for anything in my name, and I will do it. If you love me, you will obey what I command.*

There is an unfortunate paragraph division between these two verses, as if the topic has changed, but we think not. Because Jesus said often that He did and said only what the Father told Him to, these two verses belong together and form one incredible and overlooked truth. It is verified in 1 John 5:14-15:

> *This is the confidence we have in approaching God: that if we ask anything <u>according to his will</u>, he hears us. And if we know that he hears us — whatever we ask — we know that we have what we asked of him.*

When the Bible says the righteous man shall live by faith, it does not mean only that we must have faith in God. Living by faith is believing you can hear God's voice. Showing your faith is responding to what you hear, and beliving in the covenant promise of God that we will personally know and be taught by Him. It is one thing to pray a prayer with faith that God hears us, but entirely and profoundly different to hear God's own thoughts about a matter, agree with His will and speak it as a prayer in the earth to release what he has ordained in heaven. That is living by faith!

The Thoughts of God Are a Treasure

The Psalmist wrote, *I love your commands more than gold...* (Psalm 119:127)

Do we love God's commands like this — more than pure gold? Imagine you have won the lottery, and you have a ticket to millions of dollars in one hand, and the ability to hear and know God on the other, and had to choose between them. Which one would it be? Most of us will never have to make that choice. But the psalmist, who had experienced both great wealth and the voice of God, made his choice clear.

Psalm 19 agrees, saying that the thoughts, laws and ways of God are a treasure to be more desired than a large quantity of pure gold. A financial fortune may be out of the reach of most people, but the thoughts and laws of God are not. First of all, God's mind and wisdom are clearly revealed in the Bible. So we should treasure what the Bible says as if it were that financial windfall, expecting it to do the same thing we think a fortune would: give us life, happiness, and the freedom to live to our greatest potential.

But the Bible also teaches that I have free access to the thoughts of God when it says, *You have the mind of Christ.*[1] It says that if we only take time to listen for God's thoughts, if

---

[1] 1 Corinthians 2:16

we desire them more than anything, if we hunger to know how He would personally teach us, then we shall hear His words. Proverbs 2:1-5 says,

> My son, if you accept my words and store up my commands within you, turning your ear to wisdom and applying your heart to understanding, and if you call out for insight and cry aloud for understanding, and if you look for it as for silver and search for it as for hidden treasure, then you will understand the fear of the Lord and find the knowledge of God.

It is such a helpless feeling to be in virtual poverty and to feel like one has to do without the things that give one the good life. But a Christian need never have to feel that way, for he has the opportunity to receive vast treasure every morning. However, to enjoy this treasure, we first must come to value it as the Psalmist did:

> The law from your mouth is more precious to me than thousands of pieces of silver and gold. (Psalms 119:72).

We have access to this treasure; we can reach out for it and possess it. God only asks that we let it be a treasure to us, and treat it accordingly, and when He sees that we truly value it, He freely gives it to us.

How do we show that we treasure the thoughts of God? By responding to them, changing our behavior when we hear them, by holding them close in our hearts. We give Him the honor of letting Him change our minds.

Whatever God teaches you is the truth and is an expression of His perfect and unfailing love for you AND the people in your life. As we have said before, those who do not yet know this, harden their hearts. They steel themselves against hearing God's voice. Our spiritual ears "hear" only when we hold precious what God has to say, when we perk them up to listen. Those who hold no value for God's thoughts, no love of hearing His voice, will seldom seek or hear God's voice. God does not squander the great riches of His thoughts on those who do not value them.

The better you respond to God, the more you will hear.

The Bible contains a very important principle about hearing God's voice: the more you respond to what you hear from God, the more you will hear from Him. Jesus taught a lesson known as the parable of the sower, to reveal that the more we respond to God's word — both *logos* teaching and personal *rhema* breathed into our ears, the more life will be produced in and through us. As He finished teaching the parable, He usually added this warning:

> *Therefore consider carefully how you listen. Whoever has will be given more; whoever does not have, even what he thinks he has will be taken from him. (Luke 8:18)*

It is important to understand the subject here — what will we be given more of, or lose, if we don't listen? When we read this story in Matthew, the subject is made clear:

> *The knowledge of the secrets of the kingdom of heaven has been given to you, but not to them. Whoever has will be given more, and he will have an abundance. Whoever does not have, even what he has will be taken from him. (Matthew 13:11-12).*

God is trying to give us knowledge of the secrets of the kingdom of heaven. Whoever has hearing ears will be given more to listen to; whoever does not have ears to hear, even what he thinks he has will be taken from him. In other words, the person who receives knowledge from God will continue to receive more as long as he uses what he receives.

When God speaks, He expects us to respond. When a person ignores what he receives from the Lord, his voice may grow dim within that person's spirit. God will not cast His "pearls" before swine who would rather feed on slop — worldly wisdom.

The greater your measure of listening responsively, the greater your measure of hearing will be.

If you treasure hearing the words from God's mouth (and show it by responding, adjusting your life and thinking according to them) then you will hear more and more from God. But if you do not treasure His words, you may gradually lose the ability to hear His voice. The greater your measure of listening responsively, the greater your measure of hearing will be.

Remember that the Bible, even the New Testament, was written by Hebrew people. In the Hebrew culture Jesus grew up in, the concept of hearing meant more than just receiving words into the ears, it meant hearing responsively, or with the intent to obey.

Actually, culture aside, all of us are pretty much adamant about having people respond to what we say, especially our children. When you ask your child to eat his spinach and he doesn't respond, you would likely say, *Did you hear me?* Now, you are probably sitting two feet from your child; you know they heard you, so that isn't really the question. The real question you are asking is, *I know you heard me, so why aren't you obeying me?* The question is about obedience and responsiveness, not hearing.

It is the same with God, who has invited you into a divine Father-child relationship. In fact, when you show by your response that you value what He tells you, it stirs him to pour out even more of what is in His heart. Remembering that Jesus is the very personification of Wisdom,[2] consider what Wisdom says in Proverbs 1:23-28:

> *If you had responded to my rebuke, I would have poured out my heart to you and made my thoughts known to you. But since you rejected me when I called and no-one gave heed when I stretched out my hand, since you ignored all my advice and would not accept my rebuke, I in turn will laugh at your disaster; I will mock when calamity overtakes you — when calamity overtakes you like a storm, when disaster sweeps over you like a whirlwind, when distress and trouble overwhelm you. Then they will call to me but I will not answer; they will look for me but will not find me.*

Of course, Jesus would never laugh at our misfortune, but the wisdom He gives will certainly torment us if we don't follow it and suffer for it later. Have you not ignored wisdom, paid a heavy price, and later heard it "mocking" you in your thoughts?

The point is, God will not be mocked or have his counsel treated lightly. You don't repeatedly ignore God and

---

[2] According to Colossians 2:3.

expect Him to smile graciously and keep begging to talk to you. Not that he will strike you down or anything. It seems that God's favorite way to punish you for ignoring Him is to let you have what you really want:

> Since they hated knowledge and did not choose to fear the Lord, since they would not accept my advice and spurned my rebuke, they will eat the fruit of their ways and be filled with the fruit of their schemes. For the waywardness of the simple will kill them, and the complacency of fools will destroy them; but whoever listens to me will live in safety and be at ease, without fear of harm. (Proverbs 1:29-33)

The waywardness of the simple will kill them... The word translated "simple" here literally means "open, spacious, wide" and infers that one is open to all kinds of enticement, not having developed a discriminating judgment as to what is right or wrong.[3]

There can be no doubt that watching you be destroyed by walking in your own wisdom breaks God's heart, knowing that if you listen to Him you will be safe, at ease (a priceless and rare commodity) with no fear of harm. That is the state of rest we are called to in Christ. But God doesn't drop these things on you automatically, they come only when you participate with God in this relationship.

There are many wealthy people in this world. You could not expect to walk up, knock on the door of a millionaire and have him hand you a fortune. He would feel used if you tried. But if you became involved with such a man and developed an intimate relationship with him, it is entirely likely that he would share his wealth with you because of

---

[3] Theological Wordbook of the Old Testament; 1980, The Moody Bible Institute of Chicago; Page 742.

the relationship. It is no different with God and his great treasures. In covenant friendship, all wealth is freely and gladly shared.

God may not speak as an act of mercy.

If you persistently ignore God's voice through disobedience, His voice may grow muffled or fall silent within your spirit. While this can be due to a bad conscience before God, we believe that one of the main reasons for God's silence is His great mercy. God is so merciful that He won't put you in a position to be willfully sin ing against Him.

If you don't do God's will because you are ignorant or unaware of it, then you are what the Bible calls "blameless." You are not innocent, but you have not willfully sinned, and God takes that into account in His judgment. But if God reveals His will to you and you ignore it, you are then willfully sinning against Him. James said that when a man knows what to do and doesn't do it, he is consciously and deliberately sinning against the Lord.[4]   God calls this rebellion and tells us that rebellion is just as awful in His sight as practicing witchcraft.

God is merciful, and certainly not petty. He does not stop talking to you and showing you His will the minute you fail to obey a thing or two. He is a longsuffering, patient Lord and parent. It is when a Christian repeatedly fails to obey the voice of the Lord and shows no inclination to change, that His voice gradually becomes dimmer or actually confusing to the believer.

---

[4] James 4:17: *Anyone, then, who knows the good he ought to do and doesn't do it, sins.*

Eventually, we can become deceived if we consistently fail to obey what we hear from God. Deception is dangerous because a person who is deceived does not know he is decived. Our safety from deception is to fear God more than the devil, and more than our own weaknesses.

The Fear of the Lord is a Key to This Treasure

Psalm 25 reveals some important truths about who God speaks to and why:

> Good and upright is the Lord; therefore he instructs sinners in his ways. He guides the humble in what is right and teaches them his way. All the ways of the Lord are loving and faithful for those who keep the demands of his covenant. (verses 8-10)

> Who, then, is the man that fears the Lord? He will instruct him in the way chosen for him. He will spend his days in prosperity, and his descendants will inherit the land. The Lord confides in those who fear him; he makes his covenant known to them. (verses 12-14)

Consider several things the Psalmist teaches here about who God speaks to and why:

❋ He does not speak to us because we deserve it, but because He is good.

❋ He speaks to sinners when He chooses to. Hearing ears are God's gift to whoever cares to listen.

❊ He guides the humble, or those who know they need help and are looking to the Lord for guidance.

❊ Those who respond to what God says and requires of them will experience His love and faithfulness.

❊ The Lord speaks most clearly to those who reverently fear Him, even confiding in them, and making the fullest benefits of relationship (covenant) known to them.

Isaiah verifies that the fear of the Lord is a key to hearing His voice clearly:

> He will be the sure foundation for your times, a rich store of salvation and wisdom and knowledge; the fear of the Lord is the key to this treasure. (Isaiah 33:6).

He does not speak to us because we deserve it, but because He is good.

It is said that Jesus delighted in the fear of the Lord. The record that John left us of his witness of the Lord's life verifies that Jesus demonstrated His fear of the Lord by obeying everything the Father told Him. The fear of the Lord is demonstrated by submissive obedience. This is the key that unlocks the wisdom and knowledge that God wants to give to man.

If we would love God, we must hear him.

When asked to reveal the greatest command of all, Jesus replied:

> Love the Lord your God with all your heart and
> with all your soul and with all your mind. This is the
> first and greatest commandment. (Matthew
> 22:37-38).

Then in the gospel of John, Jesus says to all those who call themselves disciples:

> If you love me, you will obey what I command.
> (John 14:15)

How can we love God if we don't obey Him? And how can we obey Him if we don't hear His command?

Furthermore, if we understood how much God has prepared for those who love Him deeply, we would not hesitate to pursue it. Paul wrote:

> We speak of God's secret wisdom, a wisdom that
> has been hidden and that God destined for our glory
> before time began. None of the rulers of this age
> understood it, for if they had, they would not have
> crucified the Lord of glory. However, as it is written:
> "No eye has seen, no ear has heard, no mind has
> conceived what God has prepared for those who love
> him" but God has revealed it to us by his Spirit. (1
> Corinthians 2:7-10)

Again we have the thought of a hidden treasure: God's secret wisdom, destined for our glory, now revealed by the Spirit, who makes God's thoughts known to us.

How often we hear, "I have a mind and God expects me to use it." True, but God didn't intend for you to use your mind independent of Him. Your mind is meant to live under the influence of your human spirit, which God formed in you to be united to the Spirit of Christ, and through which you share life and can know His thoughts:

> "I have a mind and God expects me to use it."

The man without the Spirit does not accept the things that come from the Spirit of God, for they are foolishness to him, and he cannot understand them, because they are spiritually discerned. The spiritual man makes judgments about all things, but he himself is not subject to any man's judgment: For who has known the mind of the Lord that he may instruct him? But we have the mind of Christ. (1 Corinthians 2:14-16)

The phrase *the man without the spirit* in verse 14 is more accurately rendered *the natural man* in the King James Version; it is translated from the Greek word *sarx* which refers to the flesh and its natural ability to hear, see or think.

The word translated as "without" has the picture of one failing to reach out for something and take hold of it, so do not assume that this verse refers to unsaved people! Clearly, by the evidence of failed character and unhappy hearts and foolish lives, saved Christians fail to reach for the help of the Holy Spirit all too often. But it need not be. To our shame we ignore the most awesome Gift the Father is bestowing and Jesus died for us to receive.

The Spirit is always holding out what we need, and Paul is telling us that the natural soul of man does not take hold of spiritual things through his body's natural senses of hearing, sight and mental understanding. Even a saved person who tries to understand God through his natural senses rather than the senses (eyes and ears) of his spirit, will fail.

Even Jesus did not rely upon His human faculties.

Incredibly, Jesus, the perfect, sinless son of God did not rely upon His own thoughts, opinions and judgments when making decisions on how to respond to people. He said in John 8:15-16:

> You judge by human standards; I pass judgment on no-one. But if I do judge, my decisions are right, because I am not alone. I stand with the Father, who sent me.

The phrase "human standards" here is the same word, *sarx*. Jesus said that they all judged by their natural senses: their own thoughts, impressions and understanding, what they could see and hear with their natural eyes and ears. Jesus would not be like this. Isaiah prophesied of Him:

> The Spirit of the Lord shall rest upon Him, The Spirit of wisdom and understanding, The Spirit of counsel and might, The Spirit of knowledge and of the fear of the Lord. His delight is in the fear of the Lord...(Isaiah 11:2-3).

Because he delighted in the fear of God — refusing to exalt himself over Him, treating the Father's truth as the epitome of righteousness and truth — Jesus would not judge by the sight of His eyes, nor decide by the hearing of His ears. Returning to John Chapter 8, we find Jesus verifying this:

> I have much to say in judgment of you. But he who sent me is reliable, and _what I have heard from him I tell the world._ (John 8:26).

Jesus is saying in essence, "I have formed my own judgments of what is wrong with you and what I ought to say about it, but I'm not telling you my thoughts. I am listening to the voice of the Father (as the Holy Spirit reveals His thoughts to me) and that's what I share with the world. I trust my heavenly Father's judgment more than my own." He says again in verse 28: ..._I do nothing on my own but speak just what the Father has taught me._

This is a great example for every believer and for all who would minister to God's people. If the pure son of God would not rely upon His own judgments in responding to people, how dare we?

If we fail to receive the mind of Christ, we severely limit God's ability to use us. We may betray our calling to represent the heart of God rightly to the world. God wants to express Himself to others through you, and in order to do this you need to know His thoughts towards others. We can do this because we have the same Spirit that lived in Christ: the Spirit of counsel, wisdom and knowledge.

Learning To Hear His Voice

We hear God's voice with spiritual ears, not physical ones.

Reading through the gospels you find Jesus saying again and again: *He who has ears, let him hear.* When the Bible speaks of hearing God's voice, it does not mean hearing with your physical ears, but with the ears of your spirit. This often sounds very much like what we call one's "thought voice" as you "hear" in your physical mind.

This hearing is done in your human spirit. When you were born again, a new spirit was created in you, of the same essence as God's spirit, and is united with His Spirit in an everlasting relationship. Without this spirit you could not relate to God in the way the Bible promises.[1] Your human spirit can communicate through its own faculties of seeing, speaking, hearing.

Paul explains how the Spirit of God communicates God's thoughts to us:

> *The Spirit searches all things, even the deep things of God. For who among men knows the thoughts of a man except the man's spirit within him? In the same*

---

[1] Though Biblical history clearly reveals God can and will cause anyone, even heathen kings, to hear His voice when it serves his purposes.

*way no-one knows the thoughts of God except the
Spirit of God.*

*We have not received the spirit of the world but
the Spirit who is from God, that we may understand
what God has freely given us. This is what we speak,
not in words taught us by human wisdom but in
words taught by the Spirit, expressing spiritual truths
in spiritual words. (1 Corinthians 2:10b-13)*

It is by God's Spirit communicating to our spirit, that we
can understand what God has freely given us — his
thoughts, his wisdom, his truth, his counsel. We don't have
this ability because we deserve it; it is organic to every born-
again child of God, just like the ability to speak and
understand the speech of others is organic to every human
infant. Likewise, these abilities, while they live within us,
must be cultivated and practiced to help them mature.

Just like your body has eyes and ears, your spirit has the
ability to see and hear. How do we know? It is common to
hear testimonies of people who have died temporarily and
experienced the separation of their spirit and soul from their
body. (It is your spirit/soul that goes to heaven to live
eternally with God, after separating from your body at
death.) Such people speak of being able to see their own
dead body, plus seeing and hearing the other people in the
room.

Note carefully: if the physical body is dead, then the
eyes and ears of that body can no longer see and hear; it is
physically impossible. How then, does a dead person see and
hear? Through the eyes and ears of his spirit, which has a life
independent of the body. People who have "come back to
life" to tell these stories have experienced the return of their

life-spirit to their bodies when the physical body was revived.

We all have these eyes and ears in our human spirit. The problem is that most of us don't use them very well, usually because we are so busy relying upon our physical eyes and ears. In the same way that a person who becomes blind develops a much more acute sense of hearing, we need to become less reliant upon our natural eyes and ears and tune into our spirits. This is what God was referring to when he said:

> Who is blind but my servant, and deaf like the messenger I send? Who is blind like the one committed to me, blind like the servant of the Lord? You have seen many things, but have paid no attention; your ears are open, but you hear nothing. (Isaiah 42:19-20).

The Holy Spirit is broadcasting all the time, but we may not be receiving. We do not hear anything coming out of the television or radio when they are turned off, but that does not alter the fact that pictures and sounds are continually being broadcast. In order to see and hear these broadcasts, we have to turn the set (receiver) on and tune in.

The Holy Spirit is broadcasting all the time, but we may not be receiving.

Our spirits are somewhat like that. We need to tune in, and perk our ears up and listen expectantly. The Bible assures us God is speaking, and He complained through many others besides Isaiah that His people do not pay attention.

This spirit which Christ formed in you has full ability to know God no matter what is going on with your physical body. Tonia got a great lesson about this a few years ago when she was injured in an automobile accident. The concussion she suffered caused her to have temporary amnesia. She woke up in an ambulance with emergency personnel asking her if she knew who she was or where she lived. She could not think of her name or anything about herself, her husband's name or face, or where she had been going when she had the accident.

But as she lay there strapped to the body board, Tonia knew she belonged to Jesus, because His Spirit spoke to her spirit and told her she would be all right. She was so certain of this she told the ambulance workers this with calmness and certainty, feeling very peaceful and safe. Drifting in and out of consciousness, and each time Tonia awoke it was the same questions and the same response.

It would be several hours before the brain swelling went down and she regained her memory, but Tonia had unceasing communication with the Lord, who assured her that she belonged to Jesus and was safe. This was knowledge that came to her through her spirit, which was unimpaired, even though her physical brain was injured and her mind unable to function properly. Whatever she knew came only via her human spirit.

The practical steps.

Learning to hear God's voice is not difficult, Remember, God's voice is the quiet voice and may sound much like your own "thought voice." Here are three basic steps to help you:

✳ Ask God's will about whatever concerns you, sealing your prayer in Jesus' name. Philippians 4:6 says: *Do not be anxious about anything, but in everything, by prayer and petition, with thanksgiving, present your requests to God.* It is not necessary to pray about every single little thing, but by all means pray about whatever makes you anxious and when you sense it is important to know God's will.

✳ Commit to believe the first answer you hear. James 1:6-7 warns: *But when he asks, he must believe and not doubt, because he who doubts is like a wave of the sea, blown and tossed by the wind. That man should not think he will receive anything from the Lord.*

✳ Commit to trust and respond in faith to what you hear, and leave the results up to God. Don't be afraid of hearing wrongly. When God sees that you have put your faith in hearing Him and are eager to respond to what you hear, He is able to ensure that you hear His voice.

Start right now by asking: "Lord, what do you think of me?" Sit quietly and listen for the Lord's answer.

People who have trouble hearing God often don't spend enough time listening for His voice. The word picture for the Hebrew word for "hear" is a man with his two hands clasped over his mouth!

Hearing God is a lifestyle, not just a prayer time.

You don't have to set aside huge blocks of time, but develop the habit of turning aside to the Lord often as you go about your day. The Lord wants to interact with you at the kitchen sink, on the job, while you play — sharing your whole life. It is a fellowship. It's hard to imagine that what God dreamed of was having to wait every day just for that one little devoted prayer time to interact with you.

But do make room in your schedule for unhurried times with no distractions. Learn to quiet yourself and your surroundings. Begin with quiet worship, soft music or your own singing of hymns or songs to the Lord. Read your Bible, especially the Psalms, which provide a rich vocabulary for personal interaction with the Lord.

Our experience is that nearly every time we pick up the Word of God and begin to read, the Holy Spirit begins to teach. He often actually reveals things that may have nothing to do with the particular scripture being read; in some mysterious way, when one turns to the Word, the water of the Living Word begins to flow, becoming a spring of living water that is deeply satisfying. This is a significant part of what the Lord was referring to when he vowed: ...*whoever drinks the water I give him will never thirst. Indeed, the water I give him will become in him a spring of water welling up to eternal life.*[2]

If nagging thoughts persist when you are trying to pray, such as what you need to get done, jot them down on a tablet so you can dismiss them and tend to them later.

If you have a guilty conscience before the Lord, if your heart is condemning you about something, then talk to him about this first. If you have offended him or let him down, repent and ask Him to forgive you, and receive His cleansing in your spirit. People who feel guilty about something tend to avoid time with God, but you should run to Him instead, expecting to find much mercy and grace.

---

[2] John 4:14

His kindness is never more evident than when he must correct or discipline his beloved child.

And if you have not offended him, and are merely being tormented by false condemnation, then you will hear God's truth and be set free. Tonia, who has a tendency to be very hard on herself, has discovered that the Father is usually not the author of the critical thoughts she entertains in her mind. Hearing His truth has helped to set her free from a religious spirit and marvel repeatedly at the graciousness of God.

Keep a journal of your conversations with God.

Keep a journal handy at all times, and write down the thoughts which come in response to your prayers. Recording and returning to these conversations will help you remember, and show the Lord that you treasure what He is saying. It is common to begin with just one thought from the Lord, that once recorded, becomes a delightful dialogue. Furthermore, the act of writing takes the focus off of the process of hearing God, helps one to relax and enter more easily into the flow of what the Lord is saying.

Your journals will become a precious source of learning, a record of your journey with God, a touchstone for you to return to if you get lost or confused or begin to doubt.

It is a good idea to practice hearing God on small things at first. We began by praying about what to wear, what to cook, what to buy at the store...it was all a grand and delightful adventure — and still is! God had a lot of fun with us in these things, showing us His sense of humor, revealing the depth of His love in even the smallest of things in our lives. We could feel His joy in our entering this level of relationship with Him.

When Tonia was first learning this, she prayed about what to wear to a new church on one hot summer Sunday. She was given a picture of an outfit she would usually wear in fall or winter, and really thought it would be much too warm. She asked again, and was given the same picture. Though it puzzled her, Toni decided to obey in faith. It turned out that at church, the thermostat was set very low, locked in a box, and the man who had the key was unavailable! It was freezing in the building; everyone was uncomfortably cold during the service except Toni, who grinned all the time. She felt God's love in a very personal, practical way that day. You can experience God's love like this in countless ways, by listening and responding to His voice.

As noted in this example, and earlier in this book, God's answers may come in various ways, sometimes as a picture. When we ask Him what to pray about, He may speak a name or bring someone's face to mind. It is the same difference; God has communicated personally and made His will known. Yet still we cannot encourage you enough to develop an interactive, conversational relationship with the Lord. This book contains only a handful of the countless scriptures which clearly state or unmistakeably imply that God intends for this to be the normal relationship between himself and his child.

I (Ron) was recently asked this question; "Why is it important to respond to the first answer I hear?" Simply put: responding to the first thing heard is an act of faith. If you were to ask the same question over and over, you could eventually hear something easy to believe. No faith! Choosing to respond to what is first heard is your way of

saying, "Yes, Father, I choose to trust you." Remember: "...
when he asks, he must believe and not doubt...."

Trust that God is in charge of the process.

We all experience times when God is silent, or allows us
to experience our own voice or the devil's voice. But even
then He is in charge of the process, allowing this only as a
way to test, and therefore strengthen, our hearts.

Remember, we are not tested for the purpose of grading
or in order to fail. God never sets us up to fail. We are tested
only to reveal what is in our hearts — mostly to ourselves,
for God already knows. Even in this, His goal is not to catch
us doing wrong but to strengthen our faith in and
dependence upon Him. Francis Frangipane has wisely
observed that God is not interested in our perfect obedience
as much as our complete dependence.

Learn to distinguish God's voice from all others.

You must learn to recognize the voice of God through
regular, daily prayer. It is possible to hear other voices in
your spirit; you can certainly hear your own or those of evil
spirits. The loudest voice is usually your own, the quietest
one will usually be the Lord's.

It is amazing how fearful people are about hearing the
wrong voice, so much so that they would rather not try to
hear God than hear wrongly. It is as if people think God is
not powerful enough to make His voice known to them, or
that somehow he wants to make it hard for them to hear. If
you consider the history of God's pursuit of man, it is easy to
see what an absurd idea that is. It is actually an insult to the

true nature of God, which is to be the perfect father. God doesn't bestow the sound of his voice because we're mature; He makes it known to us to help us become mature.

We often hear, "I trust God; it's me I don't trust." We know the feeling, but the fact is that as a Christian, faith demands that you believe that God lives inside you by His Spirit, that you are one with Him, sharing life in all the ways that life is shared. You are, in essence, not trusting His Word when you don't trust yourself to hear Him!

> *You are, in essence, not trusting His Word when you don't trust yourself to hear Him!*

Do not shrink back in fear of messing up; God is not pleased with this. Hearing God is a very crucial part of what it means to live by faith:

> But my righteous one will live by faith. And if he shrinks back, I will not be pleased with him. (Hebrews 10:38).

Even under the Old Covenant, God said it was not difficult to receive his communication and know His will:

> Now what I am commanding you today is not too difficult for you or beyond your reach. It is not up in heaven, so that you have to ask, "Who will ascend into heaven to get it and proclaim it to us so that we may obey it?" Nor is it beyond the sea, so that you have to ask, "Who will cross the sea to get it and proclaim it to us so that we may obey it?" No, the word is very near you; it is in your mouth and in your

heart so that you may obey it. (Deuteronomy 30:11-14)

Frankly, most Christians ARE hearing from God a lot more than they realize, but just can't get comfortable with the idea of it being that simple. If you are born again and have God's Spirit in you, and have repented of any known sin, don't be overly concerned about hearing the wrong voice.

It is the Spirit of Jesus who lives in you, not the spirit of the enemy. God is the sovereign one in ultimate control. Although the devil and his demons cannot know our thoughts as God does, they are capable of communicating ideas and thoughts that our spirits can receive. If you're afraid that you may hear the voice of an evil spirit, then simply forbid that spirit to speak to you in Jesus' name. Remind him that you are one of Jesus' sheep and you can hear His voice.

Even if you do sometimes hear and respond to the wrong voice, God has allowed it for some reason which he will reveal, which is usually educational. If you respond to what you hear in faith, God will work it out. Nothing pleases Him more than seeing your faith in and hunger for His words and your efforts to obey what you hear.

Ron enjoys telling of a time in south Texas when he prayed and acted on what he heard, realizing later that he had heard wrong. He got really down on himself and was bemoaning his mistake when a church member came to visit and brought up this very action. *Pastor Ron, do you recall when you ...?* Ron replied apologetically, *Oh yes, and I'm sorry, because I really missed God on that.* The church member shook his head. *Oh no you didn't! What you did caused me to* [do a certain thing] *which is exactly what God has*

*been trying to get me to do for several days. The Lord really used
what you did to help me obey Him!*

Then Ron heard the still, small voice of the Lord say,
Romans 8:28.[3] You see, God is always looking at our hearts.
If we are sincere and serious in our attempts to respond to
Him, He assumes the responsibility of making good come
from all our prayers. When we are truly seeking God's will,
He will make sure we hear His voice.

The best guarantee of hearing rightly is loving God with
all your might. And, make it your goal to really know and
understand Him. Understanding God's heart is a safeguard
against being deceived in what you hear. Become a student
of God's character, because what He speaks will always be
consistent with his character. James refers to this fact in his
teaching letter when he says:

> But if you harbor bitter envy and selfish ambition
> in your hearts, do not boast about it or deny the
> truth. Such "wisdom" does not come down from
> heaven but is earthly, unspiritual, of the devil. For
> where you have envy and selfish ambition, there you
> find disorder and every evil practice.
>
> But the wisdom that comes from heaven is first of
> all pure; then peace-loving, considerate, submissive,
> full of mercy and good fruit, impartial and sincere.
> (James 3:14-17).

The wisdom that comes from heaven will never
contradict God's character. James makes it clear that people
who have claimed God told them to murder innocent

---

[3] *And we know that in all things God works for the good of those who love him,
who have been called according to his purpose.*

people have been deceived because of evil in their own hearts.

Anything you treasure more than God — such as a desire for revenge — can open you to deception and the thoughts of demons. Ezekiel 14:3-5 warns us that when we idolize something more than God, then He may speak to us according to our idolatry:

> Son of man, these men have set up idols in their hearts and put wicked stumbling blocks before their faces. Should I let them inquire of me at all? Therefore speak to them and tell them, "This is what the Sovereign Lord says: When any Israelite sets up idols in his heart and puts a wicked stumbling-block before his face and then goes to a prophet, I the Lord will answer him myself in keeping with his great idolatry. I will do this to recapture the hearts of the people of Israel, who have all deserted me for their idols."

This warning from God should be kept in mind by anyone who seeks "a word" through a prophet. Still, God only has one motive for allowing you to hear a word according to what you idolize, and that is to recapture your heart! But the path to that may not be too pleasant.

Don't make the Lord do it your way.

It is amazing how we approach even the Creator of the Universe as if we should be the one to determine when a conversation is going to happen and what the subject will be.

Let Him set the agenda for each prayer meeting: *Jesus, what do you want to talk about today? Who shall I pray for this morning?* If you ask questions and don't seem to get an answer, perhaps He wants to talk about something else.

Many people approach God with a set formula each day. In a living relationship every encounter is different. Some times you will be pouring out your heart to God; other times you could be listening to God pour out His. Sometimes the Holy Spirit may just want you to worship the Lord in joyful silence and drink of His joy while you walk in the sunshine. At times He will use you to intercede for others with knowledge that He gives you of their needs and what He wants to release in their lives. Often He will have you open the Bible to personally teach you. Expect to hear His voice, and let Him determine when prayer time is over. Do not pray by the hour, but by the Spirit.

> *Do not pray by the hour, but by the Spirit.*

Then when you leave the place of prayer, keep on praying. When the Word of God says pray without ceasing it is not telling us to withdraw from life like a monk, but to live a life of uninterrupted fellowship with the Lord. Develop an awareness that you are always in God's presence, that He often wants to communicate with you in the midst of your day and circumstances, not just that first hour in the morning. Praying without ceasing means being available for listening and discussing the things that interest the Lord whenever <u>He</u> wants to talk.

One realizes quickly that God does not wait for us to ask questions in order to give us direction. We cannot tell you how often spontaneous thoughts come to us when we're not even praying — which we assumed were our own, only to realize later they were God's thoughts directing us! We have missed lots of little blessings, and occasionally gotten into trouble of one sort or another by ignoring these. This is yet another application of Paul's word in 2 Corinthians 10:3-5 when he says, "...*we take captive every thought to make it obedient to Christ.*" Often those spontaneous thoughts from God are his way of showing us something he wants us to do, and we need to learn to pay attention, and not dismiss such things without asking the Lord about them.

When you're exhausted or too emotionally worked up, it is easier to have faulty hearing, and not a good time to hear God about major decisions. Powerful emotions such as anger or bitterness can block or pervert our hearing. First quiet your soul and bring yourself to rest in His presence so He can speak with you.

It is our hope that what you have read in this book will strengthen your faith and enhance your ability to have that true talking relationship "with" the Father. Never forget that his greatest desire is to communicate with you.

You will find in the final few pages, more helpful hints for hearing his voice and growing in your prayer life.

Father is waiting; don't be afraid to spend time with him and when you doubt, recall his admonition in Jeremiah:

> **"Call to me and I will answer you and tell you great and unsearchable things you do not know."**

> **Jeremiah 33:3**

APPENDIXES

A: Guidelines for Talking With God

✸ Dialogue happens only because God desires to speak. Don't force Him; learn to enjoy His presence even if He is quiet. The essence of listening is death to self. Ask Him to help you.

✸ We're like radios — sometimes our "static" (anxieties, angers, fears, business, etc.) is too noisy. If this is the case, then wait and pray for your heart to be cleansed.

✸ Don't keep asking the Lord about things you have already been given knowledge on, hoping for a different answer.

✸ Don't reduce yourself to childishness. If He has skilled you and made you wise in an area, don't keep asking Him how to do what you're doing. He wants to bring us out of servanthood into friendship and partnership. He does not want mindless slaves, and if you've developed a listening ear, He will easily break into your thoughts if He wants you to change something.

✸ When asking God for big decisions, remember He guides, but sometimes won't make the decision for you. He may let you make decisions so you can learn from them, just like we do when bringing up our children.

✸ Worship is conducive to hearing God. It is not good to blank the mind in meditation and leave it empty. When bringing your heart to quietness, meditate on God and His word, or quietly worship.

❋ Your attitude must be open towards Him. This means:

- ✓ You must be submissive.
- ✓ You must be trusting.
- ✓ You must be thankful.

B: Hindrances to Hearing God

Many times the problem lies with our side, intentionally or not, for the following reasons:

- **We really don't know God.** Read His Word, all of it!

- **Poor self-image.** "Why would God speak to me? I'm not important."

- **False sense of guilt.** True guilt stems from God, and is specific. False guilt is from Satan and is based solely on vague accusations like, "You're not good enough."

- **Busyness/Business.** We don't slow down.

- **Unbelief.** Thinking God will not speak to us personally about families, business, finances, frustrations, fears, etc.

- **God-directed Anger.** Being mad at God because He didn't do what one wanted — a spouse or child dies, bankrupty, etc. When trying to pray one can't help recall those bitter moments and just feels anger.

- **Harboring Sin.** Harboring is different from committing sin. Harboring means knowing sin is present but NOT being dealt with (resentments, angers, grudges, etc.).

- **Rebellious Spirit.** May want to pray — but doesn't really want to hear — called to repent but doesn't really want to change.

❋ **Rejecting God's Messengers.** A husband won't hear God through his wife, or the wife through her husband; or the educated won't hear through the uneducated; or won't hear from an unpleasant source. Especially ignoring authority figures: pastors, employers, judges.

❋ **Untrained to Listen.** We MUST train ourselves to listen!!

C: Hindrances to Answered Prayer

In conclusion, let's allow the scriptures to speak to some of the things which might hinder our prayers as well as some of the things, attitudes, or circumstances that might keep us from hearing the voice of the Father.

We urge you to meditate on each one, memorize these "hindrances" and whenever you are having difficulty in hearing, do a rapid review and ask which one might be applicable. Our experience is that in most cases, at least one will slap us in the face. When we repent and receive His forgiveness, we are back face-to-face once again.

1. Wrong Motives

> When you ask, you do not receive, because you ask with wrong motives, that you may spend what you get on your pleasures. (James 4:3).

What are your motives for the request you have made? Are they selfish, self-centered, or self-seeking? Is this request meant to exalt yourself or others?

2. Sin

> Surely the arm of the Lord is not too short to save, nor his ear too dull to hear. But your iniquities have separated you from your God; your sins have hidden his face from you, so that he will not hear. (Isaiah 59:1-2)

Search your heart and/or ask the Father if there is unrepentant sin in your life.

3. Unforgiveness

And when you stand praying, if you hold anything against anyone, forgive him, so that your Father in heaven may forgive you your sins. (Mark 11:25,26).

Unforgiveness may be one of the biggest hindrances. What is in your past that still hurts? Have you forgiven the one who hurt you? Are you still holding a grudge? We are commanded to forgive whether we are the one offended (Matthew 18:15) or the one who has offended another (Matthew 5:23-24).

4. Marital Difficulties

Husbands, in the same way be considerate as you live with your wives, and treat them with respect as the weaker partner and as heirs with you of the gracious gift of life, so that nothing will hinder your prayers. (1 Peter 3:7).

If the man is a tyrant, dictator, or controller; or the woman rebellious, dishonoring, refusing to submit to husband or other authority, God may NOT speak. He expects the home to be the main source of His life and leadership. If not, prayers will not be heard.

5. Satanic Resistance

Then he continued, "Do not be afraid, Daniel. Since the first day that you set your mind to gain understanding and to humble yourself before your God, your words were heard, and I have come in response to them. But the prince of the Persian kingdom resisted me twenty-one days. Then Michael, one of the chief princes, came to help me, because I was detained there with the king of Persia. Now I have come to explain to you what will happen to your people in the future, for the vision concerns a time yet to come." (Daniel 10:12-14).

6. Unbelief

"Have faith in God," Jesus answered. "I tell you the truth, if anyone says to this mountain, `Go, throw yourself into the sea,' and does not doubt in his heart but believes that what he says will happen, it will be done for him. Therefore I tell you, whatever you ask for in prayer, believe that you have received it, and it will be yours. (Mark 11:24).

But when he asks, he must believe and not doubt, because he who doubts is like a wave of the sea, blown and tossed by the wind. That man should not think he will receive anything from the Lord; he is a double-minded man, unstable in all he does. (James 1:6-8).

Very simply, God may not speak until you come to the place where you really believe that He wants to and will speak to you.

7. Disobedience

> Now it shall come to pass, IF you diligently obey
> the voice of the Lord your God... (Deuteronomy
> 28:1)

> But it shall come to pass that IF you do not obey
> the voice of the Lord your God... (Deuteronomy
> 28:15)

The entire 28th chapter of Deuteronomy states quite
clearly what happens when one obeys OR disobeys the voice
of the Lord.

8. Praying Against the Will or Character of God

> This is the confidence we have in approaching
> God: that if we ask anything according to his will, he
> hears us. And if we know that he hears us —
> whatever we ask — we know that we have what we
> asked of him. (1 John 5:14-15)

> And I will do whatever you ask in my name, so
> that the Son may bring glory to the Father. You may
> ask me for anything in my name, and I will do it.
> (John 14:13-14).

> In that day you will no longer ask me anything. I
> tell you the truth, my Father will give you whatever
> you ask in my name. (John 16:23).

Be very careful that every request, every concern is in
accordance with His will. (Example: years ago a woman

came to us wanting agreement that her lover would leave his wife so they could be married and enter ministry. Do you really think that the Lord would honor such a request?)

Study the written Word...know the written Word...and always pray according to the written Word! It is your guideline to a clear understanding and the ability to hear the voice of the Father.

Resources Available from Shammah Ministries

Books

The Woman God Designed

Leader's Guide for The Woman God Designed

Finding the Heart of God in Every Book of the Bible

Teaching on Audio & Video

Covenant: God's Pattern for Righteous Relationship

God's Plan for the Family

Entering God's Rest

Spirit Life

What Kind of Woman Will I Be?

Grace: God's Ability Within Us

The Tabernacle of Moses: A Pattern for The Priesthood of Believers

Are you Satisfied With God?

TO LEARN MORE ABOUT THESE AND OTHER PRODUCTS, LOG ONTO WWW.SHAMMAH.ORG

SEMINARS BY SHAMMAH MINISTRIES

COVENANT: GOD'S PATTERN FOR RIGHTEOUS RELATIONSHIP

SPIRIT LIFE

A COURSE FOR CHRISTIAN LOVERS

WHAT KIND OF WOMAN WILL I BE?

ENTERING GOD'S REST

For more information on how to schedule a seminar, retreat or leadership training event for your group, write to Shammah Ministries at:

shammah@charter.net

CPSIA information can be obtained
at www.ICGtesting.com
Printed in the USA
FFOW01n1748050314
4068FF